BULLET IT!
LISTS
FOR LIVING

Hello my creative readers! I can't believe I'm writing the introduction of my second notebook, BULLET IT! LISTS FOR LIVING, already!

In this new version of the book, I've created some beautiful and fun pages for you to fill out and/or color. Each page of this book is meant to inspire you to journal and express yourself through pen and paper.

This time around I'll be guiding you through different ideas and showing you unique ways in which you can use a notebook as a creative outlet, a daily planner, a personal journal, and so much more.

Just like in my first BULLET IT! notebook, I want to remind you that you should not be afraid to make mistakes in this or any other notebook you use. The most important thing is to enjoy the process of self-discovery and creative expresison.

I hope this notebook serves you well!

With love,

NICOLE LARA

WHAT TO EXPECT FROM THIS NOTEBOOK

The content of this book has been divided into sections related to different topics that are generally used in the journaling community. Next is a content list for the sections and the pages included in them:

Section 1

Personal Interests

* Favorite Reads
* Books to Read
* My Top Favorite Movies of All Time
* Movies Watchlist
* New Things I'm Eager to Learn
* DIYs & Crafts I'd Like to Try
* Places I Want to Explore
* Night Out - Favorite Spots to Go
* Spring Bucket List
* Summer Bucket List
* Autumn Bucket List
* Winter Bucket List

Section 2

Mind, Body and Soul

* Music to Make My Heart Sing
* Small Things that Bring Me Joy
* What Truly Inspires Me
* Personal Growth
* Gratitude Daily Log
* Food and Drinks Favorites
* Recipies to Try
* Goals for My Body
* Goals for My Mind
* Goals for My Heart
* Me Day
* Positive Affirmations

Section 3

Memory keeping

* Inspiring People
* Favorite Family Vacations
* A Day in a Line

Section 4

Play

* Brainstorm List
* Planner Icons
* Color Code
* Planner Doodles
* Favorite Pens Swatch
* Favorite Washi Tape Swatch

Section 5

Life Planning

* Where Do I see Myself in 10 Years?
* Life Goals
* Goals Planning
* Year Calendar
* Yearly Tasks
* Monthly Tasks
* Monthly Pages
* My Ideal Week
* Weekly Tasks
* Time is on Your Side
* Morning and Night Routine

How to use this notebook?

As you can see from the previous list, each section of this notebook contains pages that are related to a specific aspect of life and planning.
Each page has a prompt and instructions on how to fill out the page. However, there are no restrictions on how you can use each page included in this book. Feel free to experiment with the layouts and change any aspect of them.

At the end of each section and the notebook there are blank pages for you to use freely. You can expand any of the ideas already included to create your own spreads.

so grab your
favorite pens
and let's start
creating!

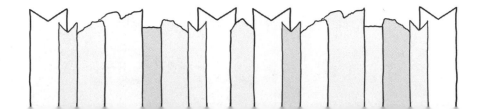

favorite

Use this page to write down the books you love most. You can write them down in a ranked list or jot them down as you remember them!

My favorite books

My favorite authors

My favorite book quotations

reads

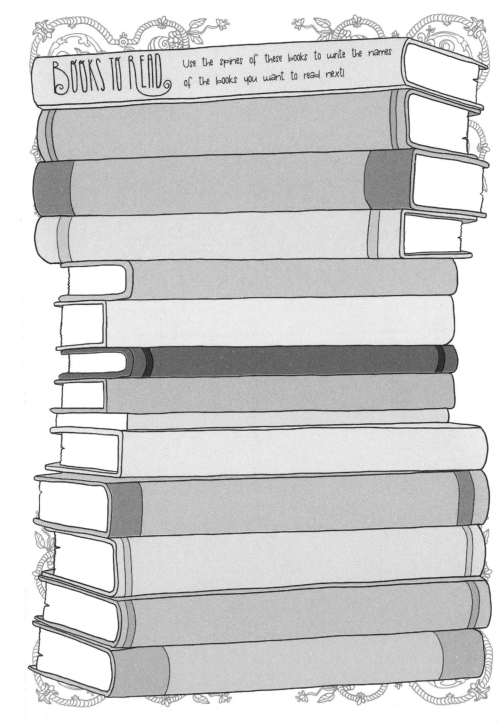

BOOKS TO READ

Use the spines of these books to write the names of the books you want to read next!

MY TOP

FAVORITE MOVIES OF ALL TIME

IT'S SHOW TIME! Make a list of your favorite movies of all time and rank them from 1 to 10!

1.
2.
3.
4.
5.
6.
7.
8.
9.
10.

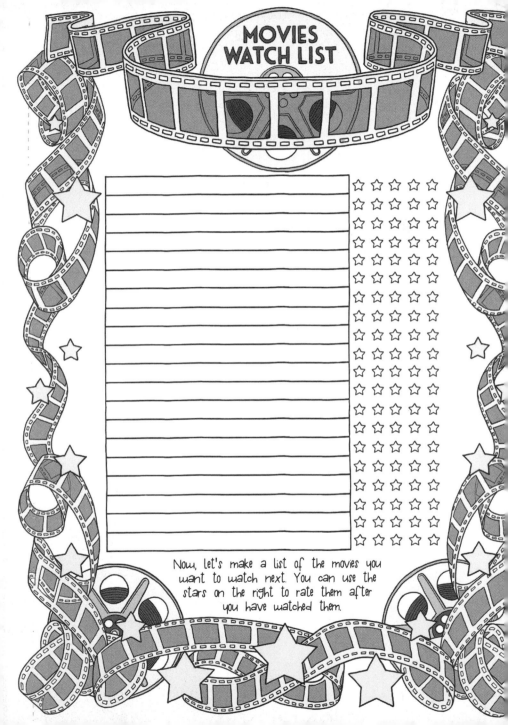

MOVIES WATCH LIST

☆ ☆ ☆ ☆ ☆
☆ ☆ ☆ ☆ ☆
☆ ☆ ☆ ☆ ☆
☆ ☆ ☆ ☆ ☆
☆ ☆ ☆ ☆ ☆
☆ ☆ ☆ ☆ ☆
☆ ☆ ☆ ☆ ☆
☆ ☆ ☆ ☆ ☆
☆ ☆ ☆ ☆ ☆
☆ ☆ ☆ ☆ ☆
☆ ☆ ☆ ☆ ☆
☆ ☆ ☆ ☆ ☆
☆ ☆ ☆ ☆ ☆
☆ ☆ ☆ ☆ ☆
☆ ☆ ☆ ☆ ☆
☆ ☆ ☆ ☆ ☆
☆ ☆ ☆ ☆ ☆
☆ ☆ ☆ ☆ ☆
☆ ☆ ☆ ☆ ☆
☆ ☆ ☆ ☆ ☆

Now, let's make a list of the movies you want to watch next. You can use the stars on the right to rate them after you have watched them.

New Things I'm Eager to Learn

You're never too old to learn new things! Write down three things you want to learn this year in each of the bubbles. You can also specify how you're going to learn them and when you plan to start.

DIYs & CRAFTS

I'd like to try

Now it's time to get crafty.
Make a list of DIYs and crafts
you have always wanted to
make on the washi tapes.

PLACES I WANT TO EXPLORE

List places you would like to travel someday soon!

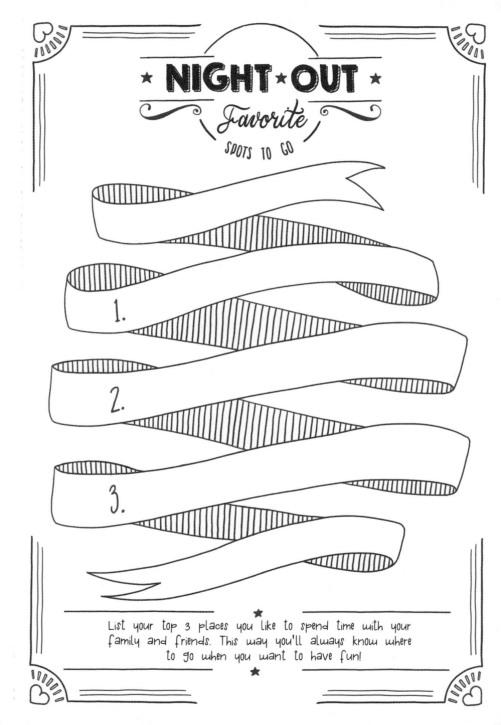

★ NIGHT ★ OUT ★

Favorite

SPOTS TO GO

1.

2.

3.

List your top 3 places you like to spend time with your family and friends. This way you'll always know where to go when you want to have fun!

Spring Bucket List

Use this and the next three pages to list all the fun things you want to do during each season.

Summer Bucket List

Autumn Bucket List

Winter Bucket List

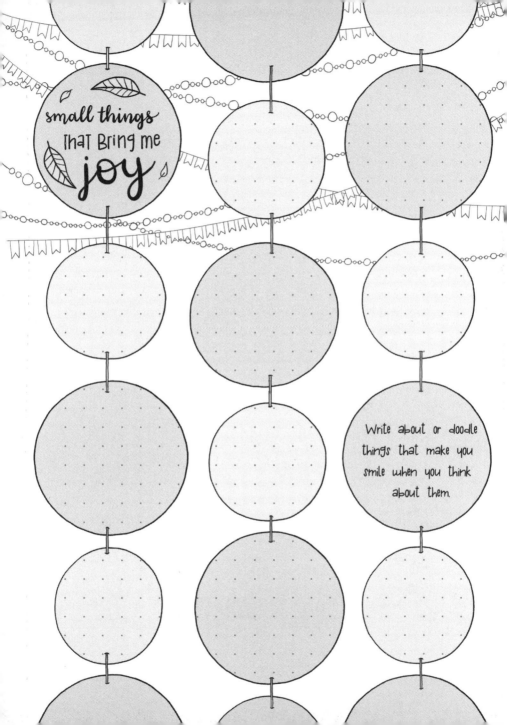

small things
that Bring me
joy

Write about or doodle
things that make you
smile when you think
about them.

WHAT TRULY INSPIRES ME

When we feel inspired, we live with more passion and determination. Write about what inspires you to keep moving forward. Come back to this page whenever you need an inspiration boost.

PERSONAL GROWTH

List 10 qualities you want to cultivate that will help you become a better version of yourself.

gratitude

DAILY LOG

"Gratitude unlocks the fullness of life"

- Melody Beattie -

Starting each day with a grateful heart is an essential part of bringing happiness to your life. Write down at least one thing you are grateful for each day and color one of the lotus petals. Watch as the beautiful lotus blooms with each passing day.

①

②

③

④

⑤

⑥

⑦

⑧

⑨

⑩

(11)

(12)

(13)

(14)

(15)

(16)

(17)

(18)

(19)

(20)

(21)

(22)

(23)

(24)

(25)

(26)

(27)

(28)

(29)

(30)

Food and Drinks

Let's make a list of foods you can't live without!

Recipes

TO TRY

Why not take these favorite foods and create fun recipes with them?

GOALS FOR MY BODY

Make a list of short-term and long-term goals you have for your overall health. What practices will help you feel confident and healthy?

GOALS FOR MY MIND

Now let's make a list for goals for you mind. What will spark your creativity, clear your mind, strengthen your memory, or boost your productivity?

GOALS FOR MY HEART

Make a list of short-term and long-term goals for your heart. What will fill you with love for yourself and others?

me day

It's really important to have a day or part of a day to refresh your body, mind and spirit. Make a list of things you'd like to do during that time that can help you relax and unwind.

♥
♥
♥
♥
♥
♥
♥
♥
♥
♥
♥
♥
♥

positive affirmations

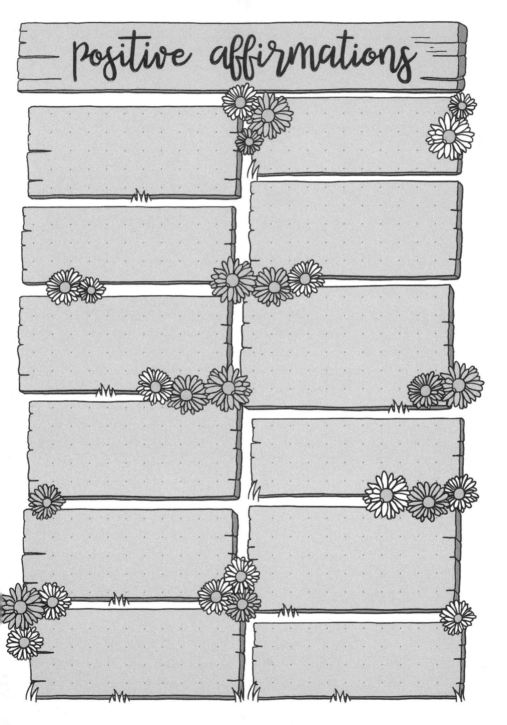

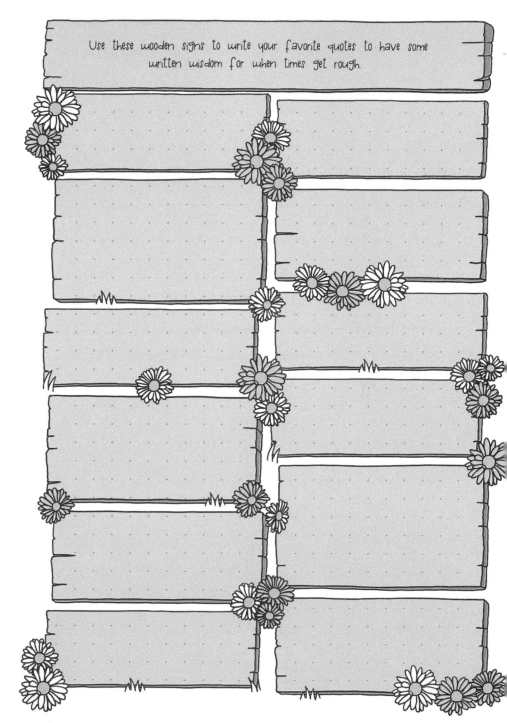

Use these wooden signs to write your favorite quotes to have some written wisdom for when times get rough.

Inspiring people

The people in our lives and the relationships we build help us to learn and grow. Who are five people who have influenced and inspired you along your personal journey? Write or doodle about them inside each frame.

FAVORITE *family* VACATIONS

Now let's remember the best times with our family and friends. Doodle, write or stick a picture of your favorite vacations with the people you love the most.

a day IN A line

Create a day-to-day memory story of your year! Fill in these monthly pages with anything you like. As you jot down one idea, tidbit, or event from each day, you'll narrate the whole story of your year.

january

1
2
3
4
5
6
7
8
9
10
11
12
13
14
15
16
17
18
19
20
21
22
23
24
25
26
27
28
29
30
31

february

1
2
3
4
5
6
7
8
9
10
11
12
13
14
15
16
17
18
19
20
21
22
23
24
25
26
27
28
29

march

1
2
3
4
5
6
7
8
9
10
11
12
13
14
15
16
17
18
19
20
21
22
23
24
25
26
27
28
29
30
31

april

1
2
3
4
5
6
7
8
9
10
11
12
13
14
15
16
17
18
19
20
21
22
23
24
25
26
27
28
29
30

may

1
2
3
4
5
6
7
8
9
10
11
12
13
14
15
16
17
18
19
20
21
22
23
24
25
26
27
28
29
30
31

june

1
2
3
4
5
6
7
8
9
10
11
12
13
14
15
16
17
18
19
20
21
22
23
24
25
26
27
28
29
30

july

1
2
3
4
5
6
7
8
9
10
11
12
13
14
15
16
17
18
19
20
21
22
23
24
25
26
27
28
29
30
31

august

1
2
3
4
5
6
7
8
9
10
11
12
13
14
15
16
17
18
19
20
21
22
23
24
25
26
27
28
29
30
31

september

1
2
3
4
5
6
7
8
9
10
11
12
13
14
15
16
17
18
19
20
21
22
23
24
25
26
27
28
29
30

october

1
2
3
4
5
6
7
8
9
10
11
12
13
14
15
16
17
18
19
20
21
22
23
24
25
26
27
28
29
30
31

november

1
2
3
4
5
6
7
8
9
10
11
12
13
14
15
16
17
18
19
20
21
22
23
24
25
26
27
28
29
30

december

1
2
3
4
5
6
7
8
9
10
11
12
13
14
15
16
17
18
19
20
21
22
23
24
25
26
27
28
29
30
31

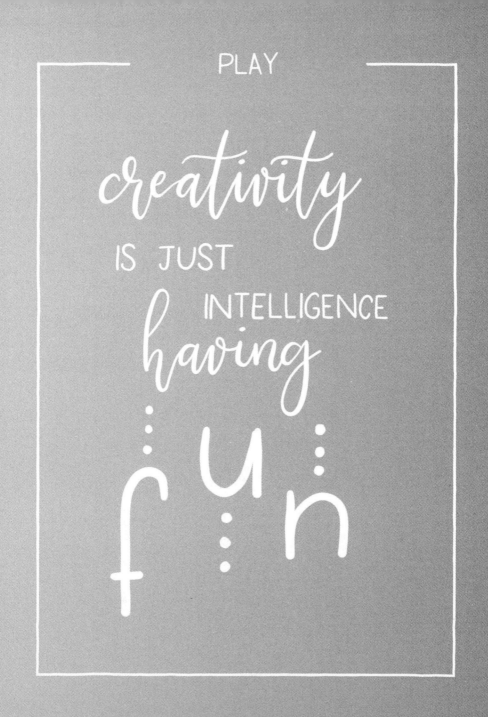

BRAINSTORM
list

Great ideas always come at the most unexpected times. For this reason, always keep your notebook close so you can make a list of these ideas here!

PLANNER ICONS

Using symbols to plan will help your brain remember those important tasks. Use this box to draw simple yet remarkable symbols to use with your tasks and events.

COLOR CODE

A color-coding system consists of classifying different tasks and events into colors so you can easily identify and remember them when planning. Examples of categories can be work, personal tasks, health, self-care, etc. Combining these with your planner icons will give you the tools to have a functional planner system in no time!

planner doodles

Use these boxes to draw some doodles you'd like to use to decorate your planner pages. These can be functional doodles like boxes and banners, or purely decorative ones. Choose whatever you like the best!

planner doodles

FAVORITE *pens* SWATCH

Let's create an inventory of your favorite pens. You can refer to this page later on to choose what pens to use on your different pages.

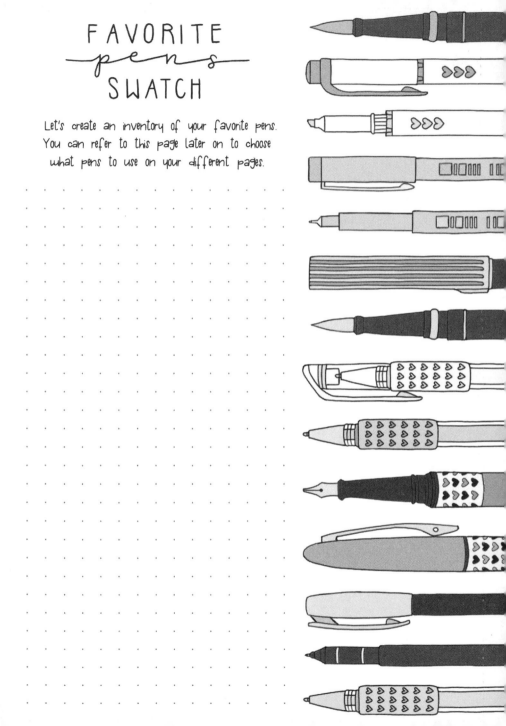

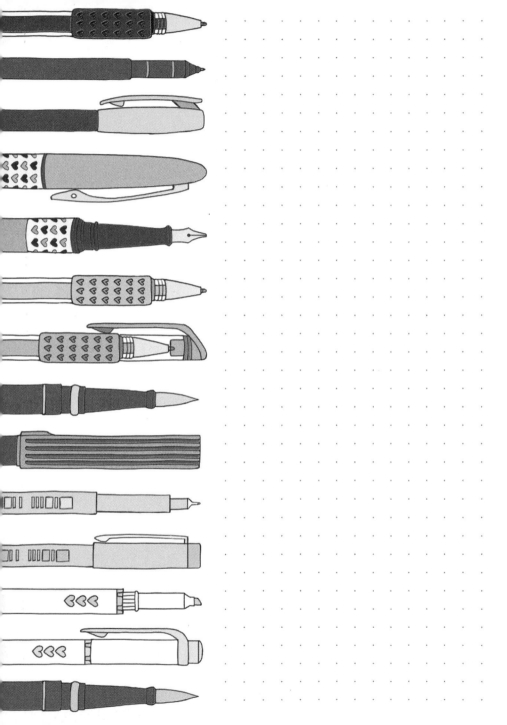

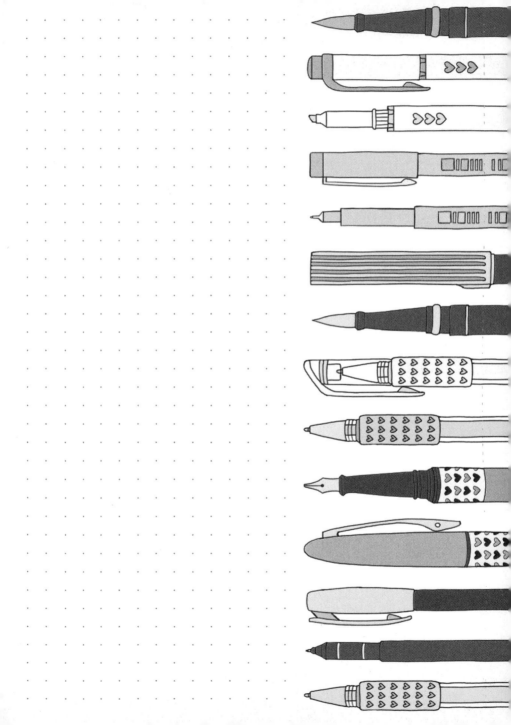

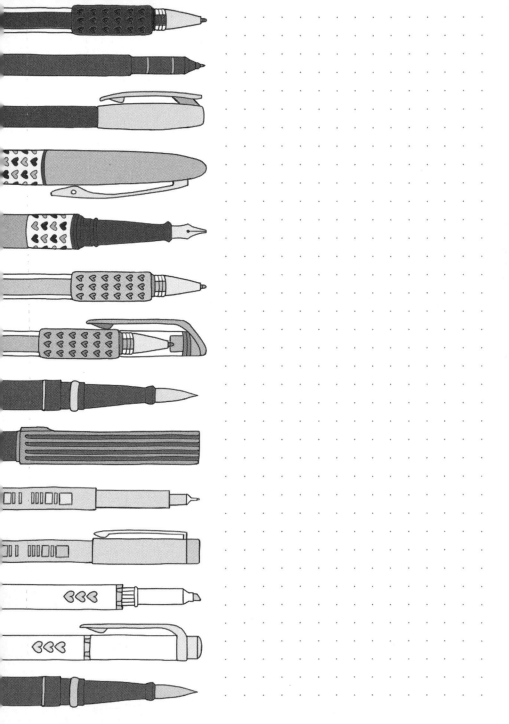

washi tape swatch

Put your favorite washi tapes in the boxes below. This list will help you decide how to combine them when decorating your pages.

LIFE PLANNING

A
Goal
WITHOUT A
Plan
IS JUST A
Wish

WHERE DO I SEE MYSELF 10 years?

Now that we've had a ton of fun writing about the things we enjoy the most, let's get a bit more serious to start planning our days for a better future.

Before the planning can begin, we must know what our main aspirations are. This future vision of yourself will guide you every month, week, and day so you can move forward with purpose.

On the left page, fantasize about what your future self in 10 years will be like. What are you doing for a living? Where do you live? What do you do in your free time? Answer these and any other questions that come to mind.

life goals

life time

Are you done journaling your heart out? Then you're ready to start crafting some goals that will take you to that future self you fantasized about.

goals

PERSONAL

CAREER

FINANCIAL

FUN / BUCKET LIST

RELATIONSHIPS

Use what you wrote to create 1 to 2 life goals for each category included above.

5 year plan

PERSONAL

CAREER

FINANCIAL

FUN / BUCKET LIST

RELATIONSHIPS

Take your life goals and get more specific by writing what you want to get accomplished by the 5-year mark.

1 year plan

PERSONAL

CAREER

FINANCIAL

FUN / BUCKET LIST

RELATIONSHIPS

Let's be even more specific and break down the goal into smaller goals for every year.

monthly action

PERSONAL

CAREER

FINANCIAL

FUN / BUCKET LIST

RELATIONSHIPS

What do you have to do every month of the year that will ensure you accomplish your yearly goals?

daily action

PERSONAL

CAREER

FINANCIAL

FUN / BUCKET LIST

RELATIONSHIPS

Success is about daily action. Specify one small action you must do every day to accomplish your bigger goals.

Goals Planning

Now it's time to take the goals you wrote before and break them down with the goal planning worksheets on the following pages. These worksheets are divided into the following sections:

GOAL NAME AND DESCRIPTION
This section is to define the goal. Always be as descriptive as possible when describing your goals.

3 MAIN ACTION STEPS AND DEADLINES
With a clear idea of what your goal is, you can create a list of the 3 most important steps you should complete to reach your goal. Give these steps a deadline to keep you accountable.

RESOURCES NEEDED
What resources do you need to achieve your goal? Make a list of the resources you have and the ones you need to get.

GOAL TO-DO LIST
Break down your 3 main action steps into baby steps to create an actionable to-do list.

At the end of the worksheet, there's some white space to write extra notes or to-dos.

GOAL WORKSHEET

GOAL NAME

GOAL DESCRIPTION

3 MAIN ACTION STEPS

1

2

3

RESOURCES NEEDED

GOAL TO-DO LIST

GOAL DEADLINES

FINISH BY

GOAL WORKSHEET

GOAL NAME

GOAL DESCRIPTION

3 MAIN ACTION STEPS

1

2

3

RESOURCES NEEDED

GOAL TO-DO LIST

GOAL DEADLINES

FINISH BY

GOAL WORKSHEET

GOAL NAME

GOAL DESCRIPTION

3 MAIN ACTION STEPS

1

2

3

RESOURCES NEEDED

GOAL TO-DO LIST

GOAL DEADLINES

FINISH BY

GOAL WORKSHEET

GOAL NAME

GOAL DESCRIPTION

3 MAIN ACTION STEPS

1

2

3

RESOURCES NEEDED

GOAL TO-DO LIST

GOAL DEADLINES

FINISH BY

january
m t w t f s s

february
m t w t f s s

march
m t w t f s s

april
m t w t f s s

may
m t w t f s s

june
m t w t f s s

july
m t w t f s s

august
m t w t f s s

september
m t w t f s s

october
m t w t f s s

november
m t w t f s s

december
m t w t f s s

yearly tasks

Use the calendar on the left to write down the dates of the year your using this notebook in. Then, write down tasks you have to do in a yearly basis (or every couple of months) on this list to be able to check them off when you complete them.

J F M A M J J A S O N D

monthly tasks

Use the preset lists below to write down tasks or events that have to be done or occur every month.

Monthly Pages

Creating monthly pages is a great way of staying organized and productive throughout the month. That's why the next layouts I've created are dedicated to this. The pages include the following sections:

monthly calendar

1 🎂 Mary's Birthday!
   👕 Laundry day.
2 ♡ No work! Invite John for dinner

Use this calendar to schedule events and important tasks.
Use your color and symbols system too!

monthy habit

1	2	3	4	5	6	7	8	9	10
11	12	13	14	15	16	17	18	19	20
21	22	23	24	25	26	27	28	29	30
31	workout								

Write the days of the month inside the boxes and use them to mark off the days you complete your habit.

monthly goals and to-do list

Use the dotted boxes to write a goal list and to-do list.

word of the month

Write an inspiring word for the month to motivate you to move forward.

monthly notes

Use the blank space to write monthly notes or a monthly review.

The pages were left uncolored so you can have fun coloring each month with your favorite colors!

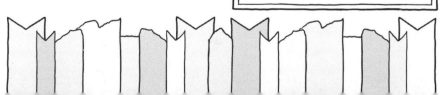

January

·1·	·11·
·2·	·12·
·3·	·13·
·4·	·14·
·5·	·15·
·6·	·16·
·7·	·17·
·8·	·18·
·9·	·19·
·10·	·20·

monthly notes

word of the month

monthly habit

·21·

·31·

·22·

monthly to-dos

·23·

·24·

·25·

·26·

·27·

·28·

·29·

·30·

month goals

February

monthly calendar

1

2

3

4

5

6

7

8

9

10

11

12

13

14

15

16

17

18

19

20

monthly notes

word of the month

monthly habit

21

22

23

24

25

26

27

28

29

30

month goals

31

monthly to-dos

march

monthly calendar

1

2

3

4

5

6

7

8

9

10

11

12

13

14

15

16

17

18

19

20

monthly notes

word of the month

monthly habit

21

22

23

24

25

26

27

28

29

30

31

monthly to-dos

month goals

april

monthly calendar

· 1 · · · · · · · ·
· 2 · · · · · · · ·
· 3 · · · · · · · ·
· 4 · · · · · · · ·
· 5 · · · · · · · ·
· 6 · · · · · · · ·
· 7 · · · · · · · ·
· 8 · · · · · · · ·
· 9 · · · · · · · ·
· 10 · · · · · · · ·

· 11 · · · · · · · ·
· 12 · · · · · · · ·
· 13 · · · · · · · ·
· 14 · · · · · · · ·
· 15 · · · · · · · ·
· 16 · · · · · · · ·
· 17 · · · · · · · ·
· 18 · · · · · · · ·
· 19 · · · · · · · ·
· 20 · · · · · · · ·

monthly notes

word of the month

monthly habit

21

22

23

24

25

26

27

28

29

30

31

monthly to-dos

month goals

may

monthly calendar

· 1 ·
· 2 ·
· 3 ·
· 4 ·
· 5 ·
· 6 ·
· 7 ·
· 8 ·
· 9 ·
10 ·

11 ·
12 ·
13 ·
14 ·
15 ·
16 ·
17 ·
18 ·
19 ·
20 ·

monthly notes

word of the month

monthly habit

21 _____

22 _____

23 _____

24 _____

25 _____

26 _____

27 _____

28 _____

29 _____

30 _____

month goals

31 _____

monthly to-dos

June

monthly calendar

1 _____

2 _____

3 _____

4 _____

5 _____

6 _____

7 _____

8 _____

9 _____

10 _____

11 _____

12 _____

13 _____

14 _____

15 _____

16 _____

17 _____

18 _____

19 _____

20 _____

monthly notes

word of the month

monthly habit

21

22

23

24

25

26

27

28

29

30

31

monthly to-dos

month goals

july

monthly calendar

1

2

3

4

5

6

7

8

9

10

11

12

13

14

15

16

17

18

19

20

monthly notes

word of the month

monthly habit

21

22

23

24

25

26

27

28

29

30

month goals

31

monthly to-dos

august

monthly calendar

1 _____ 11 _____

2 _____ 12 _____

3 _____ 13 _____

4 _____ 14 _____

5 _____ 15 _____

6 _____ 16 _____

7 _____ 17 _____

8 _____ 18 _____

9 _____ 19 _____

10 _____ 20 _____

monthly notes

word of the month

monthly habit

21 _____
22 _____
23 _____
24 _____
25 _____
26 _____
27 _____
28 _____
29 _____
30 _____

month goals

31 _____

monthly to-dos

september

monthly calendar

1 · · · · · · · · · · ·   11 · · · · · · · · · · ·

2 · · · · · · · · · ·   12 · · · · · · · · · · ·

3 · · · · · · · · · ·   13 · · · · · · · · · · ·

4 · · · · · · · · · ·   14 · · · · · · · · · · ·

5 · · · · · · · · · ·   15 · · · · · · · · · · ·

6 · · · · · · · · · ·   16 · · · · · · · · · · ·

7 · · · · · · · · · ·   17 · · · · · · · · · · ·

8 · · · · · · · · · ·   18 · · · · · · · · · · ·

9 · · · · · · · · · ·   19 · · · · · · · · · · ·

10 · · · · · · · · · ·   20 · · · · · · · · · · ·

monthly notes

word of the month

monthly habit

21

22

23

24

25

26

27

28

29

30

month goals

31

monthly to-dos

october

monthly calendar

1 · · · · · · · · · · · ·
2 · · · · · · · · · · · ·
3 · · · · · · · · · · · ·
4 · · · · · · · · · · · ·
5 · · · · · · · · · · · ·
6 · · · · · · · · · · · ·
7 · · · · · · · · · · · ·
8 · · · · · · · · · · · ·
9 · · · · · · · · · · · ·
10 · · · · · · · · · · · ·

11 · · · · · · · · · · · ·
12 · · · · · · · · · · · ·
13 · · · · · · · · · · · ·
14 · · · · · · · · · · · ·
15 · · · · · · · · · · · ·
16 · · · · · · · · · · · ·
17 · · · · · · · · · · · ·
18 · · · · · · · · · · · ·
19 · · · · · · · · · · · ·
20 · · · · · · · · · · · ·

monthly notes

word of the month

monthly habit

21 _____

22 _____

23 _____

24 _____

25 _____

26 _____

27 _____

28 _____

29 _____

30 _____

31

monthly to-dos

month goals

november

1 _____

2 _____

3 _____

4 _____

5 _____

6 _____

7 _____

8 _____

9 _____

10 _____

11 _____

12 _____

13 _____

14 _____

15 _____

16 _____

17 _____

18 _____

19 _____

20 _____

monthly notes

word of the month

monthly habit

21

22

23

24

25

26

27

28

29

30

month goals

31

monthly to-dos

december

monthly calendar

1 ⋯⋯⋯⋯⋯⋯⋯⋯⋯⋯⋯⋯⋯⋯

2 ⋯⋯⋯⋯⋯⋯⋯⋯⋯⋯⋯⋯⋯⋯

3 ⋯⋯⋯⋯⋯⋯⋯⋯⋯⋯⋯⋯⋯⋯

4 ⋯⋯⋯⋯⋯⋯⋯⋯⋯⋯⋯⋯⋯⋯

5 ⋯⋯⋯⋯⋯⋯⋯⋯⋯⋯⋯⋯⋯⋯

6 ⋯⋯⋯⋯⋯⋯⋯⋯⋯⋯⋯⋯⋯⋯

7 ⋯⋯⋯⋯⋯⋯⋯⋯⋯⋯⋯⋯⋯⋯

8 ⋯⋯⋯⋯⋯⋯⋯⋯⋯⋯⋯⋯⋯⋯

9 ⋯⋯⋯⋯⋯⋯⋯⋯⋯⋯⋯⋯⋯⋯

10 ⋯⋯⋯⋯⋯⋯⋯⋯⋯⋯⋯⋯⋯⋯

11 ⋯⋯⋯⋯⋯⋯⋯⋯⋯⋯⋯⋯⋯⋯

12 ⋯⋯⋯⋯⋯⋯⋯⋯⋯⋯⋯⋯⋯⋯

13 ⋯⋯⋯⋯⋯⋯⋯⋯⋯⋯⋯⋯⋯⋯

14 ⋯⋯⋯⋯⋯⋯⋯⋯⋯⋯⋯⋯⋯⋯

15 ⋯⋯⋯⋯⋯⋯⋯⋯⋯⋯⋯⋯⋯⋯

16 ⋯⋯⋯⋯⋯⋯⋯⋯⋯⋯⋯⋯⋯⋯

17 ⋯⋯⋯⋯⋯⋯⋯⋯⋯⋯⋯⋯⋯⋯

18 ⋯⋯⋯⋯⋯⋯⋯⋯⋯⋯⋯⋯⋯⋯

19 ⋯⋯⋯⋯⋯⋯⋯⋯⋯⋯⋯⋯⋯⋯

20 ⋯⋯⋯⋯⋯⋯⋯⋯⋯⋯⋯⋯⋯⋯

monthly notes

word of the month

monthly habit

21

22

23

24

25

26

27

28

29

30

month goals

31

monthly to-dos

MY IDEAL week

monday

12	1	2	3	4	5	6	7	8	9	10	11
12	1	2	3	4	5	6	7	8	9	10	11

Use the time trackers and the blank space to write down what your ideal week would be like.

This is a perfect chance to use the planner icons and color-coding system you created previously!

thursday

12	1	2	3	4	5	6	7	8	9	10	11
12	1	2	3	4	5	6	7	8	9	10	11

friday

12	1	2	3	4	5	6	7	8	9	10	11
12	1	2	3	4	5	6	7	8	9	10	11

tuesday

12	1	2	3	4	5	6	7	8	9	10	11
12	1	2	3	4	5	6	7	8	9	10	11

wednesday

12	1	2	3	4	5	6	7	8	9	10	11
12	1	2	3	4	5	6	7	8	9	10	11

saturday

12	1	2	3	4	5	6	7	8	9	10	11
12	1	2	3	4	5	6	7	8	9	10	11

sunday

12	1	2	3	4	5	6	7	8	9	10	11
12	1	2	3	4	5	6	7	8	9	10	11

weekly tasks

Make a list of the tasks you have to perform every week. Come back to this page every week to make sure you complete all your weekly tasks.

time is on your side

Make a list of small daily tasks you can perform in the time frames below. This will give you an idea of what to do when you have some spare time or during breaks.

5-10 mins

10-15 mins

_____

_____

_____

_____

_____

_____

15-20 mins

20-25 mins

_____

_____

_____

_____

_____

_____

morning
ROUTINE

Let's figure out what our perfect days would look like. Routines help us by giving our days structure, and making us more efficient at doing tasks we must do repetitively.

For this reason, let's create a morning and night routine that will help you start off the day with lots of positive energy and then relax and recover for the next day to come.

night
ROUTINE

The morning is the best time to be productive and to get the most important tasks of the day done. Make a list of things you can do every morning to prepare your mind and body for a new day.

As the day comes to an end, we want to make sure our bodies are relaxed and ready for a good night sleep. Make a list of things you can do every night to ease your mind and relax your body.

Congrats! You've finished your BULLET IT! LISTS FOR LIVING notebook. I've left some blank pages on the back for you to use as you wish. See ya!